Edition Eulenburg

Fräulein Delphine von Schauroth gewidmet

CONCERTO

G minor

for

Pianoforte and Orchestra

by

Felix Mendelssohn-Bartholdy

Op. 25

First performed 17th October, 1831, at Munich

with Mendelssohn at the Piano.

Foreword by
MAX ALBERTI

Ernst Eulenburg, Ltd. London, W.1.
Edition Eulenburg, G.m.b.H., Zurich
Edition Eulenburg, K.-G. Stuttgart
Eulenburg Miniature Scores, New York

PRINTED BY THE SOHO PRESS, LONDON, W.I.

MENDELSSOHN'S
PIANO CONCERTO NO. 1
G. MIN. OP. 25

Mendelssohn's reputation as a prodigy was not only based on his quality as a composer, but as well and even more as a pianist. He had appeared since his 10th year, but not yet with a composition of his own in a greater style, when he, in the autumn of 1830, during a year's stay for studies in Rome, conceived the idea of writing a Piano Concerto, which «I would like to write to myself for Paris, is beginning to whirl in my head.» We then lack to learn much about the origin of the work. Not before October 6th 1831 he reports from Munich about an imminent, great charity concert, containing only his own compositions, among which «a new Piano Concerto». This concert took place on October 17th in the presence of the king and queen of Bavaria. He first conducted some of his orchestral works and then, as per a letter from the following day «I came to my Piano Concerto and met with a long and vivid reception. After my playing they tried to call me back and applauded, as it is usual here, but I was modest and did not appear again.»

Also the following performances, as far as is known to us, saw him as the soloist: first Paris, then London and after his return Leipzig, where he introduced himself to the Gewandhaus, the place of his forthcoming activities. In Paris, where he was fostered by the then leading conductor Habeneck, he became acquainted with Liszt, who was 2 years younger, and he submitted to him the new work. Liszt played it through at sight from the irreadable manuscript. An extraordinary success was reserved for him in London on 28th May. As a result the concert was repeated on 18th June. Mendelssohn was then already known and popular in England from a previous visit. The periodical «Athenaeum» calls the Concerto «a dramatic scene for the Piano and the performance an astonishing exhibition for Piano playing».

MENDELSSOHN
KLAVIER-KONZERT NR. 1
G-MOLL OP. 25

Mendelssohns Ruf als «Wunderkind» beruhte nicht nur auf seiner Eigenschaft als Komponist, sondern auch und sogar in erster Linie als Pianist. Seit seinem zehnten Jahre war er als solcher aufgetreten, aber noch nie mit einer eigenen Komposition größeren Stils, als er im Herbst 1830, während eines etwa einjährigen Studienaufenthaltes in Rom, den Plan faßte, ein Klavier-Konzert für seine eigenen Aufführungen zu schreiben. Am 16. Oktober berichtet er darüber: «Auch ein Klavier-Konzert, das ich mir für Paris gern schreiben möchte, fängt an, mir im Kopf zu spuken.» Wir hören dann nicht viel über die Entstehung des Werkes; erst am 6. Oktober 1831 berichtet er aus München über ein bevorstehendes großes Wohltätigkeitskonzert, das nur Kompositionen von ihm, darunter «ein neues Klavier-Konzert» enthalten sollte. Dieses Konzert fand am 17. Oktober in Gegenwart des bayerischen Königspaares statt. Er dirigierte erst einige seiner Orchesterwerke und, um einen Brief vom folgenden Tage zu zitieren: «Dann kam ich zu meinem Klavier-Konzert und wurde lebhaft und lange empfangen. Sie wollten mich nachher hervorrufen und klatschten, wie es hier Mode ist; aber ich war bescheiden und kam nicht».

Auch die nächsten Aufführungen, soweit sie uns bekannt sind, wurden von ihm selbst ausgeführt: zunächst Paris, dann London und nach seiner Rückkehr Leipzig, wo er sich beim Gewandhaus, seiner künftigen dauernden Wirkungsstätte, damit einführte. In Paris, wo er durch den damals führenden Dirigenten Habeneck gefördert wurde, lernte er den zwei Jahre jüngeren Liszt kennen und legte ihm das Werk vor. Liszt spielte es sofort aus dem kaum leserlichen Manuskript vom Blatt vollkommen durch. Besonders groß scheint der Erfolg am 28. Mai 1832 in London gewesen zu sein; denn das Konzert wurde bereits am 18. Juni wiederholt. Mendelssohn war da-

C. 1

Owing to these successes the publishers Breitkopf and Härtel, Leipzig, made up their minds to publish the parts at once. The fact, that the score was not printed until long after Mendelssohn's death in 1862, was not contrary to the practice of that time.

The work is none of those, which had founded Mendelssohn's fame even if he had written nothing else, such as f. i. the Violin Concerto. But it contributed much to cement the reputation he had gained with the works of his youth; and it is, even though often misused by hands of dilettants, still an essential element of the programmes of our time. It must in no way be considered as stale or out-of-date.

It should be mentioned, that a strong inspiration was exerted by Weber's «Konzertstück» in F min. even though, contrary to this work, no programmatic character whatever is inherent. A distinct sign of this influence is recognisable from the immediate sequal of the movements. This is a form aspired and cultivated by Mendelssohn in several other works, which, however, was premature to his time. In a letter of 28th December 1833 he calls the work «a quickly sketched matter»; and this fact explains after Mendelssohn's biographer E. Wolff «the uniformed spirit and elan of this masterpiece, the artistic achievement of which is equal to its popularity».

The dedication to the young pianist Delphine von Schauroth (born 1813 at Magdeburg), with whom Mendelssohn became acquainted in Summer 1830 at Munich before his Italian journey, does not say that the work was designed for her. It ist known however, that she later on, long after Mendelssohn's death, played the Concerto publicly, f. i. in 1870 at a Mendelssohn memorial in the Gewandhaus, Leipzig.

January 1950.   Max Alberti.

mals schon von einer früheren Reise her bekannt und populär in England; die Zeitschrift «Athenaeum» nannte das Konzert «eine dramatische Szene für Klavier» und die Aufführung «eine erstaunliche pianistische Leistung».

Auf Grund dieser Erfolge entschloß sich der Verlag Breitkopf & Härtel, Leipzig, sofort die Stimmen herauszugeben. Daß die Partitur erst lange nach Mendelssohns Tode, 1862, erschien, ist bei der damaligen Praxis nichts Außergewöhnliches.

Das Werk gehört nicht zu denen, die Mendelssohns Ruhm auch dann begründet hätten, wenn er sonst nichts geschrieben hätte, wie etwa das Violin-Konzert. Aber es hat doch sehr dazu beigetragen, den Ruf, den er mit seinen Jugendwerken errungen hatte, zu befestigen, und es ist, wenn auch vielfach von Dilettantenhänden mißbraucht, doch bis heute ein Bestandteil der Konzertprogramme geblieben; es kann in keiner Weise als abgestanden oder veraltet angesehen werden.

Es verdient erwähnt zu werden, daß eine starke Anregung von Webers Konzertstück in f-moll ausgegangen war, wenn auch, im Gegensatz zu diesem Werk, kein irgendwie programmatischer Charakter vorliegt. Ein deutliches Zeichen dieses Einflusses ist zu erkennen an der unmittelbaren Folge der Sätze, eine Form, die Mendelssohn auch bei zahlreichen anderen Werken am Herzen gelegen hat, mit der er aber seiner Zeit weit vorausgeeilt war. In einem Brief vom 28. Dezember 1833 nennt er das Werk «ein schnell hingeworfenes Ding», daraus erklärt sich nach Mendelssohns Biographen E. Wolff «der einheitliche Schwung und Zug dieses Meisterstücks, dessen Kunstvollendung seiner volkstümlichen Wirkung die Waage hält».

Die Widmung an die junge Pianistin Delphine von Schauroth (geb. 1813 in Magdeburg), die Mendelssohn im Sommer 1830 vor seiner italienischen Reise in München kennengelernt hat, bedeutet nicht, daß das Werk für sie bestimmt gewesen wäre. Aber es ist bekannt, daß sie später, noch lange nach seinem Tode, das Konzert öffentlich gespielt hat, u. a. bei einer Mendelssohn-Feier im Leipziger Gewandhaus im Jahre 1870.

Januar 1950.   Max Alberti.

Piano Concerto

1

Felix Mendelssohn-Bartholdi, Op.25
1809-1847

Ernst Eulenburg Ltd.
London – Zurich – Stuttgart.

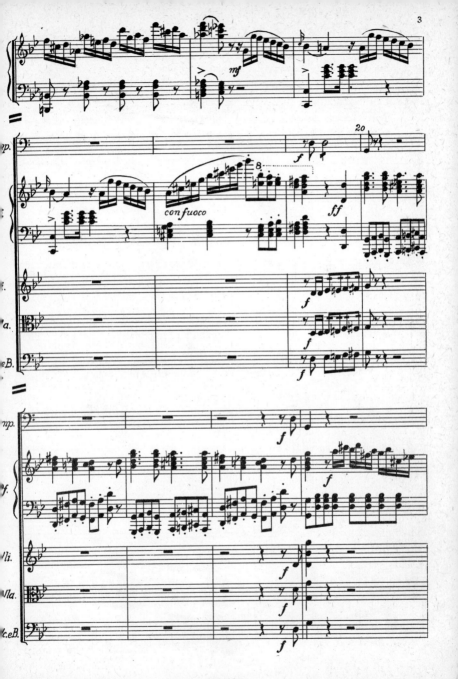

E.E.6011

9

E.E.6011

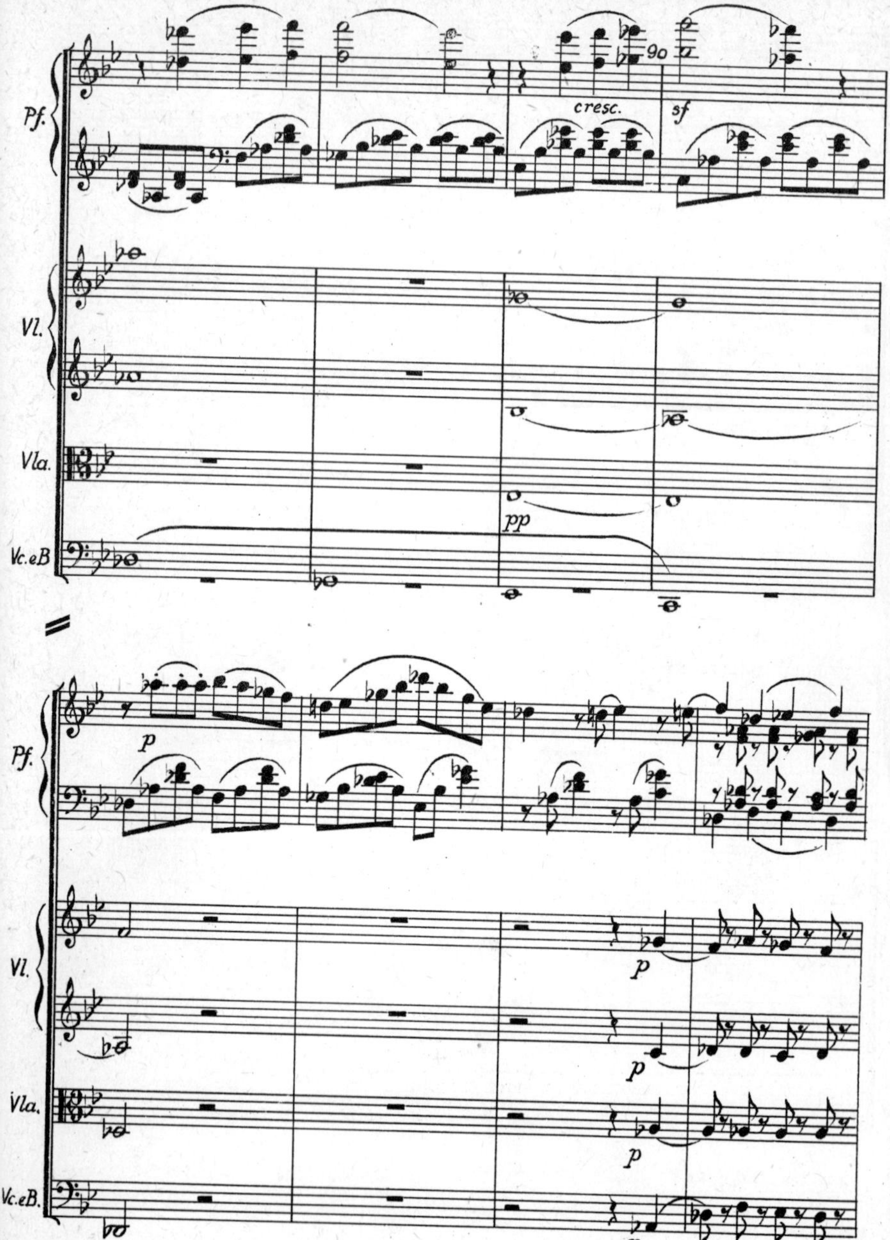
Pf.
Vl.
Vla.
Vc.eB
90
cresc.
sf
pp
Pf.
p
Vl.
p
p
Vla.
p
Vc.eB.
p

21

26

E.E.6011

32

E.E.6011

48

E.E.6011

E.E.6011

51

E.E.6011

II

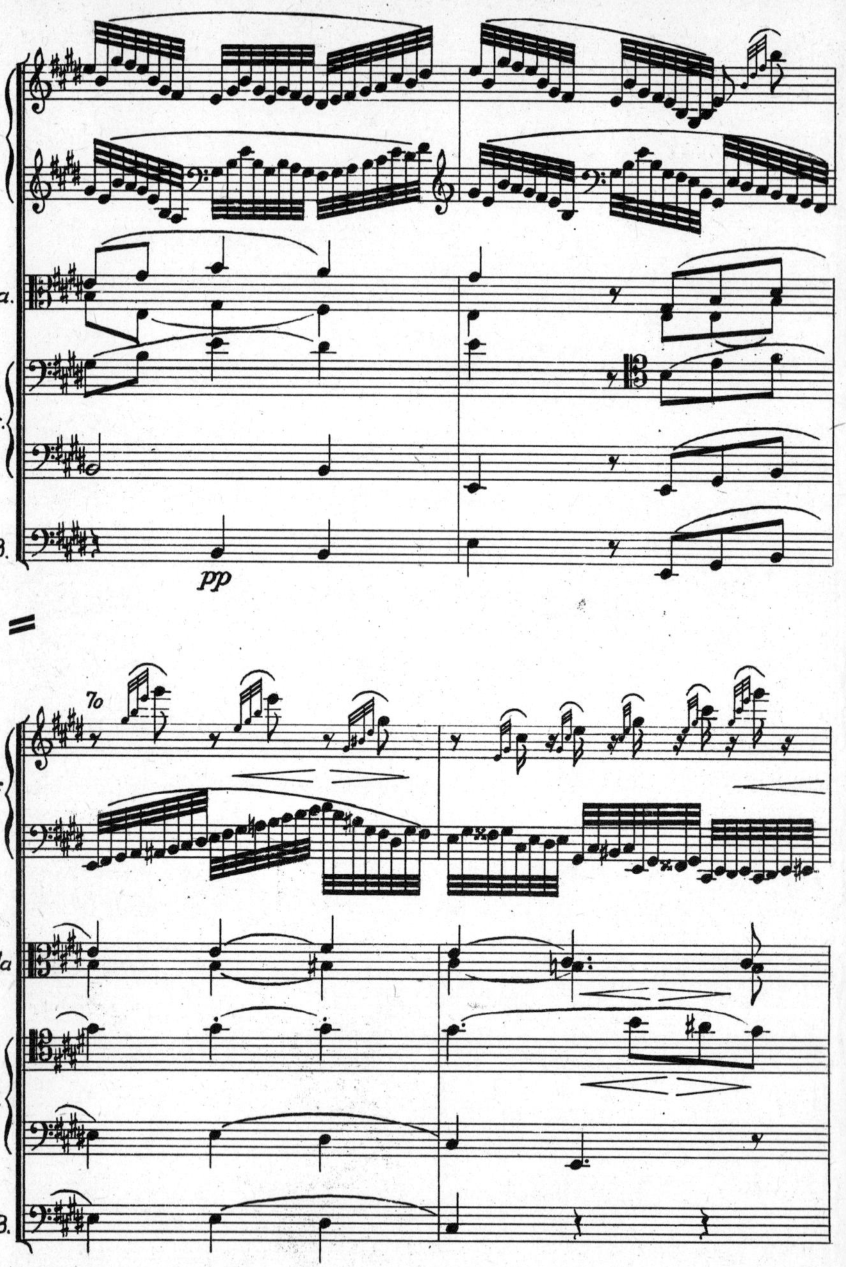
Pf
Vla.
Vc.
B.
pp
70
Pf
Vla
Vc.
B.

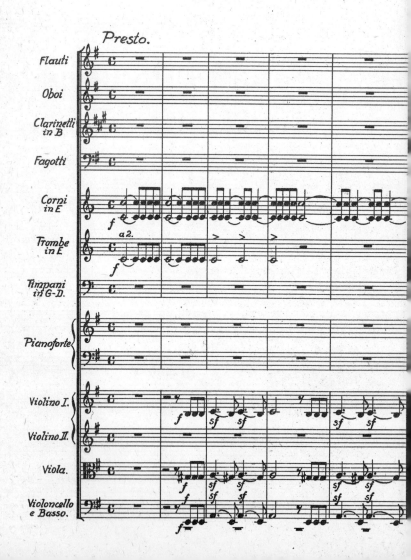

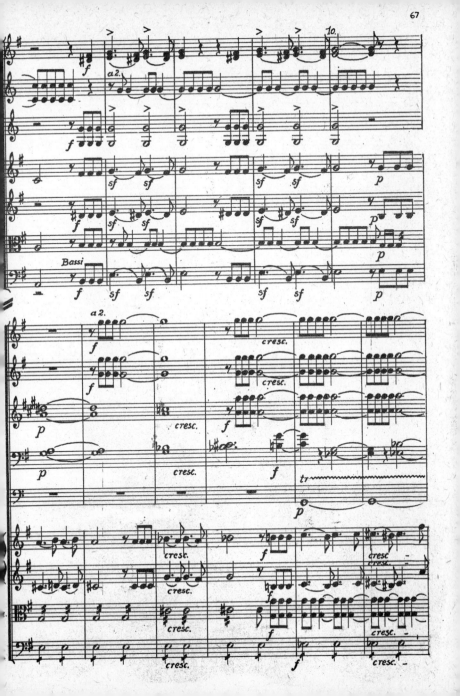

72

E.E.6011

Molto allegro e vivace.

70
Pf.
cresc
dim.
p
ritard.
a tempo
p leggiero
pizz.
Vl.
pizz.
Vla.
pizz.
Vc. e B.
pizz.
Pf
Pf
sf

92

E.E.6011

103

E.E.6011

110

116

E.F.6011

122

123

E.E.6011